So That's What 70 Looks Like!

Elegantly Endorsed

Bobbie is one of the most charismatic and resilient people I've ever met! She has a joy for life and learning that is absolutely contagious. This book is filled with fascinating stories and priceless life advice. It's a great read! Bobbie digs deep within herself to examine life's lessons and shares what she's learned with humor and grace. There's something here for every adult. May we all be as fabulous when we hit our 70s!

—**Carole Smith,** Marketing Executive, Non-Profit Board Member. Friend since 1994

Bobbie makes each year look better than the last. Her book *So, That's What 70 Looks Like!* puts a new perspective on ageism. We've heard "age is just a number," and Bobbie is a shining example. This book is one to share with your daughter, nieces, and girlfriends. Thank you, Bobbie, for being such an inspiration to women across the world. We don't need to fear getting older. We can get excited about it!

—**Keri Murphy,** Entrepreneur and Video Marketing Expert
CEO, The Inspired Living Company
Be Seen, Be Known, Be Paid for Your Brilliance through IL's IT Factor On-Camera training

As a loved and nurtured child of The Greatest Generation, I had countless heroes and role models whose sacrifices and accomplishments still astonish me. But one thing my parents, who were pillars of selflessness, could not model for me was self-care and self-awareness, which in today's world are the mandatory foundations of physical, mental, and emotional survival. Your book provides a template for us to mold who we ARE with who we CAN be. The stories of your childhood, the bricks and dumpster, your heritage, teaching children to swim while simultaneously finding themselves, coaching others as to how they present themselves to the world, and many others, provide vivid lessons and lasting encouragement for living and loving in this century. The images in the book are fun and instructive. The galley has me GLOWING!

Congratulations! As we SOUTHERN Italians would say, Buona Fortuna!

—**Vince Corica,** Executive Coach, Writer, Speaker

Former SVP at Equifax and graduate of the United States Military Academy at West Point

This gem of a book is both a work of art and a doorway to the core essences of your soul. Whether you are a young woman or beyond 70 years of age, Bobbie's inimitable style, humor, and wisdom will show you how to embrace your own style in the world you inhabit—internally by clarifying your values and externally by showcasing your various "essences." Life isn't about "looking younger" but aging graceful, and Bobbie Casalino-Lewis is the master and mentor of doing just that!

—**Baeth Davis,** Aka Dr. Purpose, YourPurpose.com

Bobbie has always been an irrepressible force! This read is fabulously true and honest. She has put forth, with tremendous effort, her journey of self-exploration. A refreshing "shot in the arm," this book is a must-read for anyone; her life's anecdotes will touch you.
—**Angela Oliveri,** Friend since 1979

No matter what season of life you are in, you will find value in this book. There are so many mysteries in life. It's important to be clear on what matters. The insights shared can help you with that. In the author's words: ***Happily-ever-after is a work in progress, and now you have a partner.*** Yes, indeed. The perfect balance of purpose and play as you discover your own steps in the dance.
—**Kathi Cooper Laughman,** Author, Speaker, Strategist
Bringing purpose to the forefront of business

Special mention to **Bonnie St. John** who you will see has been a tremendous inspiration for me in life and this project. She's a very special lady. "Thanks for mentioning me! Looks great. I wish you the best of luck on this project. I'm sure it will be a big hit and help many people! Big hugs, Bonnie"
Speaker and Author of *Live Your Joy, How Great Women Lead,*
Micro Resilience, and *How Strong Women Pray*
Graduate of Oxford University and Harvard University, The Bishop's School

Aging is inevitable, and women, especially, dread it and try to do everything they can to hide it. What I love about the portraits in this book is that Bobbie Casalino-Lewis shows how aging gracefully can be beautiful and very powerful. With age comes wisdom and a special freedom that we can express joyfully; you can see that joy and power exude through her images. Bobbie shows a side of beauty that is real and attainable for all those who choose to embrace all the special moments on their journey. The side captions and behind-the-scenes stories of the photos also show us how Bobbie overcame negative experiences in her life and chose to become a victor, not a victim. This lesson is about more than beauty through all ages. It is about demonstrating acceptance and forgiveness through all stages of our lives. If you're looking for a way to transform negative feelings about aging into opportunities for growth, this book is a good source. It's for anyone who wants to rise above the challenging stigma of natural aging and succeed while being at peace with who they are, both inside and out. Bobbie refuses to be defined by adversity and instead finds empowerment. She will help you embrace your resilience and define true beauty. One of my favorite quotes is by Audrey Hepburn:

"The beauty of a woman is not in a facial mode but the true beauty in a woman is reflected in her soul.

It is the caring that she lovingly gives, the passion that she shows.

The beauty of a woman grows with the passing years."

I feel the essence of this message throughout all the images.

—**Crystal Oculee**, Chief Financial strategist, Confidence Wealth Management

"Reading a book about vibrant maturity is refreshing in a society that worships youth. Bobbie's positive mindset is inspiring. Disarmingly authentic, she has fully embraced her divine feminine. Her effervescent spirit leaps from the page into my heart, and her story provides a blueprint for abundant living. I recommend this book to everyone."

—**Carol Koppelman,** Author, *Do the Necessary: Let The Rest Go To Hell*
Director, Park Lane Jewelry

So That's What 70 Looks Like! is an excellent resource for women of all ages. Showing there is grace in all stages of life. Standing true to who you are is a gift to envelop. We were selected to be leaders for a women's networking group called Lifestyle. Told, "You two together would be powerful." Here we are, seven years later, magnetically drawn together by other forces and joyfully calling each other woo-woo sisters. I have three words for Bobbie. Magnetic – Divine – Playful.

—**Luanne Casillas,** Retirement Specialist

Bobbie's book gives great insight into life's journey and how to keep it all in perspective. Most importantly, everyone's journey belongs to them and no one else. Her adventuresome soul combines with her kindness and is a breath of fresh air. This book has a little something for everyone, no matter your age. Love her honesty, love the book – Bobbie inspires me to live my dreams!

—**Gwen Vuchsas,** Woman Business Owner, SECO Investigations,
Founder, Playa Venice Sunrise Rotary Club, Past Honorary Mayor, Westchester, CA

So That's What 70 Looks Like! is a wonderful book for all ages. In fact, the earlier in your life that you read it, the more time you have to use Bobbie's wisdom to help you in your own life. After coming out of a pandemic, I think people need this book more than ever to help them live their best lives. We have all learned, especially these past few years, that we don't know how long we will live on this earth. As I grow older, I grow wiser and realize that life is too short not to be your true self, your best self, find joy in every day, and live life to the fullest. This book motivates me in the next chapter of my own life. Bobbie's personal insights and stories so inspire me. With her book,  she can mentor us all. Bobbie is a truly amazing woman in so many ways! I hope to look, act, and feel like her when I turn 70, and as she does, I want to GLOW!

—**Mary-Catherine (MC) Micka,** Television Producer
Director of Business Relations at the LAX Coastal Chamber of Commerce

 Bobbie Casalino-Lewis lights up every room she enters. No one takes your inner glow and brings it to life on the outside better than her. Bobbie was instrumental in getting me "Red Dot" ready for my TEDx talk in Manhattan Beach, California. How I looked on stage reflected precisely how I felt inside when I walked inside the red dot: EUPHORIC! Bobbie knew from the moment she met me exactly how to make me appear approachable with that touch of uniqueness that truly captured my core value as a CATALYST: wearing my Survivor Buff! Bobbie is a one-of-a-kind, and after reading this book, you will feel the GLOW she exudes in every aspect of her life.

—**Rich Keller,** CATALYST Effect Officer, SCORE, Helping entrepreneurs step into their identity in 'One Word'!

So That's What 70 Looks Like!

The Essence of Aging Gracefully

Bobbie Casalino-Lewis

Goodyear, Arizona

Printed in the United States of America in 2023 by Bobbie Casalino-Lewis

Paperback ISBN: 978-1-958405-75-8
Hardcover ISBN: 978-1-958405-74-1
eBook ISBN: 978-1-958405-76-5
Library of Congress Control Number: 2023906091

Publishing House: Spotlight Publishing House™ in Goodyear, AZ
https://spotlightpublishinghouse.com
Editor: Lynn Thompson, Living on Purpose Communications
Book Cover Design: Becky Norwood, portrait photographer Gervel Sampson
Interior Design: Marigold2k
Portrait Photographer: Gervel Sampson Photography at gervelsampson.com
Portrait Photographer: Megan Pagoda, Pogoda Visuals
Branding & Marketing Specialist: Chelsea Marie
Wardrobing: Bobbie Casalino-Lewis
Contact: https://bobbiecasalinolewis.com

Dedication

All women younger and older than I am

Three very special ladies I have had
the joy and opportunity to mentor,
Hayley Krawitz, Kari Jaffe, and Dina (Casalino) Skinner

Beau Saul-James Lewis

Dale Lewis

Foreword

by Baeth Davis

When Bobbie Casalino-Lewis first came into my view, we were at a networking meeting in Manhattan Beach, California. It was love at first sight. But not the romantic kind. The role-model kind. Deep in my gut, I just "had" to know her. Bobbie has this power—and she sure has it with me—to, in a moment, render one speechless, awed, and awakened to Truth. I've seen her have the same influence on people from the stage, at networking events, in mastermind meetings, and over lunch.

If I recall correctly, Bobbie's outfit highlighted her sparkling blue eyes. She wore a blue and white striped top configured at an angle over her slim hips, legs clad in white jeans, and feet sporting some saucy low heels with bows. Her hair was wildly curly in a thoughtful way, and she had on colorful horn rim glasses and red lipstick. She was radiant. I can't remember a time when she hasn't been glowing. While some folks dress to impress and sometimes intimidate, I could sense Bobbie dressed for her joy and to bring joy to others. And joy oozed out from her experienced, I-can-not-tell-a-lie gaze. This woman was not someone you could easily fool, nor was she just out to "get leads" for her business. Instead, she was in service to something larger than herself—to the Truth and Beauty of Life.

Bobbie later told me she had a similar experience when she saw me. A feeling of soul recognition, a feeling that something more was to unfold between us, the "what" and the "how" unknown and irrelevant. Life would show us why we were brought together—and life has indeed been showing us a path to greater self-understanding, self-awareness, self-compassion, joyful friendship, and respect.

It's been nearly five years since our first meeting, and I am delighted to be writing the foreword to her magnificent gem, *So That's What 70 Looks Like: The Essence of Aging Gracefully.* This book is more than a fashion guide or a how-to manual, not exactly a memoir nor a tell-all, either—it's a delicious glimpse into one woman's soul and an opportunity to look more fully into your own. Bobbie shares the "essences" of her life as a way of explaining the larger meaning of what it is to be your authentic self, to be a woman, and to live according to your own inner "triangle" of values. (Bobbie shares her inner value triangle in the book, so you can make your own if you'd like.) I suspect this book would make Carl Jung proud, for it is also about archetypes—the different ways your soul expresses itself—depending on the circumstances, both expected and unexpected. Bobbie calls these archetypes "essences." Through short, often hilarious, and deeply moving stories and exquisite, original photographs taken by Gervel Sampson, Bobbie role-models 12 archetypal essences so that you have an opportunity to identify and express your own core essences and find the courage to express yourself with the world through your value system and your style.

For example, her "Gladiator" essence features a photo of Bobbie decked out in summer gladiator style with the two German Shepherds she shares with her husband, Dale. You can see the joy and confidence Bobbie exudes as well as the kindness from her value triangle emanating from the photo. You can also see that this woman has boundaries, and her nature commands respect. All from ONE photo! The Kind Gladiator. A new spin on the gladiator, eh?

The way we "dress" internally and externally can make us or break us, and Bobbie explains through her wisdom and experience a "way through" life that is joyful, creative, and uniquely stylish.

I encourage you to grab a cup of your favorite beverage and set aside a couple of hours of your time to read this book cover to cover. That's all it takes to re-ignite your soul with a passion for your own journey, a journey only you can take, a journey into your core essences with Bobbie as your mentor and guide.

This reading treasure has already sparked some new ideas for me in how I can "show up" with more visibility and authenticity at home and at work in my core essences. May it do the same for you!

To Your "Essential" Purpose,
Baeth Davis, aka Dr. Purpose, YourPurpose.com
Aberdeen, NJ, USA

Introduction

Every year for my birthday, I do something new, unique, daring, and always fun. Turning 70, I had tremendous plans to travel with a bunch of other septuagenarian gals to foreign shores, specifically Greece. I had tried to go there at 40, but through multiple extenuating circumstances, such as the war in Iraq, I didn't go. Around that same time, our fairy godmother, Lily Campbell-Rose, introduced my future husband and me shortly before my 40th birthday. So, I changed my plans from going solo to the outer Greek islands in nothing more than a bikini to an unforgettable barefoot cruise with him on the Phantom, a late 1700s Schooner around the Grenadines. So here I was again, Greek Isle deprived. What to do? I woke up, slapped my leg, and said, "I am going to write a book! Not just any book about random stuff, but a book that women and enlightened men would purchase, read, inscribe, and pass on to their children, and daughters in particular."

In addition to satisfying my desire to mark my 70th birthday in a new and more innovative way than ever, it seemed time to commit my story, or the essential highlights, from my heart to paper.

So, I called Becky Norwood of Spotlight Publishing House, my client, friend, and now publisher, whose look, life, and confidence I transformed in front of an entire roomful of people at an event in Scottsdale, Arizona, in 2017. The next call was to Gervel Sampson, the photographer of the incredible images in this book. I didn't get ten words out of my mouth about my idea before she said, "I Am Your Gal," and was she ever. We collaboratively planned and shot every photo in this book in ONE DAY—Gervel and I flowed from photograph to photograph with wordless precision. I wardrobed myself. Imagine eating your own cooking and liking it! Before you knew it, we had all the right-wrong combinations to depict my essence in each chapter.

Becky introduced me to my editor, Lynn Thompson whose patience and tenacity has steered me through new waters into a wonderful collaborative relationship, like we are in a two-woman boat. Since I started this book, I've taken up yet another endeavor: rowing. I joined the Los Angeles Rowing Club (LARC). Eight-seat boat plus coxswain, an exquisite (very) early-morning activity requiring teamwork, cadence, collaboration, and rhythm, with ninety-percent women.

For a while now, I have repeatedly heard, "You are HOW old? Get out of here, no way. You look like this or that age!" So, I got to thinking, other than being lucky in the gene pool (my father had fabulous skin), I have a perpetual, youthful curiosity.

I discovered late in the game that finding a role model was futile. As a child, young woman, and age-of-wisdom gal, I was haunted by the desire to have a role model. Oh, there were plenty of role models, but they were outside of my reach; none of them were up close up and personal who could and would stroke my hair and say, "You are beautiful, you are smart, you are loved, and you can do, be, and aspire to any damn thing you want."

I surrendered the search and realized I had enough experience to qualify for self-mentoring. So, I hired myself! I would be my own role model while being one for all the women in my life younger than me who showed up by chance or choice. Why not? Being 70, most women I knew or heard about had already thrown themselves on the scrap heap of life—what the hell? How could that be when I felt 70 was the new 20, just a lot wiser?

After thoroughly enjoying my 60s and entering my 70s feeling vital with more joy and clarity than ever, please don't think for a split second it was easy—oh hell no. Therapy, messiness, loveless childhood, failed relationships, a divorce, second marriage, motherhood, body issues, family drama, sibling rivalry insanity, parental care battles, ooh fah, and managing my journey of marriage and raising a beautiful human, my son, Beau Saul-James Lewis.

My life purpose is to impact as many women as possible to feel better about themselves regardless of age. I do have an affinity for Millennials and creating gap-bridging conversations. We are the bookends of this time and have exceptional gifts to share. Of course, I can only have personal interactions with so many women. However, I can pave the road via this book and speak on large-audience platforms to share what got me over the hump. The euphemism that creates the most significant visual for me is that I am paving over potholes in my life so those who come after me don't have to sink into the same holes. To arrive at 70 happy with who I am, vibrant, wise, and joyful, it was incumbent on me to at least share how I did it.

Carl Jung said: "The greatest burden of a child is the unlived life of their parent."
That is not happening on my watch!

"I'm at that wonderful juncture in life where I'm old enough to have experience
and young enough to remember it."
—Bobbie-ism

Table of Essences

Discovering my essences at a two-day workshop was a big part of my adult self-realization process. Several folks gathered in the iconic Larchmont area of Los Angeles, where as a group, we dug into the essences, discovering our individualized versions. It was an unforgettable venture into self-discovery with the help of others holding up the mirror and providing input. The conclusion was a deeper meaningful understanding of who I am and how I am perceived. I curated and painstakingly assembled a collage of images depicting all of my essences. I had the board luxuriously matted (in navy suede) and substantially framed to seal and protect the contents. Believe it or not, the framing cost more than the course; however, I knew this piece would be in my life forever. Every day this beautiful creation hangs on the wall across from my desk to perpetually remind me to be true to who I am. The list of Essences with my versions:

Leadership – Fellowship

Dark Side – Constrained

Inner Child – Buoyant

Passion – Animated

Dramatic – Exuberant

Humor – Mischief

Romantic – Glamorous

Sensual – Coquette

Braced – Spontaneous

Spiritual – Simple

Inner Male – Gladiator

Grace – Comfort

Leadership – Fellowship

Essence is Leadership
My Version of Leadership is Fellowship

Being born in the sign of Leo and the oldest of four children, leadership was a given, but the question was, what style of leader was natural for me? Ever since I was a little girl, I have bridged people together, typically from very different aspects of my life, to create community through fellowship. Fellowship is a friendly association, especially with people who share interests. I have been very intentional in developing my gift and ability to get inside people and see their uniqueness and what is at their core to make meaningful connections. By understanding their essence, I can assemble the building blocks of community. That's how I lead.

In my Vice President days in the 1980s at IPC (Interconnect Planning Corp) on Wall Street, I led and retained a 28-member Project Management Team that hummed for a decade. What was challenging and unique was 27 members were female—and only one male. This team navigated all-male trade unions, specifically Local Three Electrical Union, AT&T, New York Telephone Company, and multiple service providers, to deliver 100% quality installations on time every time. Each team member had specific skills that I paired with specific companies—it was like orchestrating a symphony. This highly talented team of attractive women managed the installations of all the major stock, bond, and futures trading rooms in the brokerage business. In their beautiful outfits and high heels, they skillfully wove together all aspects of the projects. They went from sawdust on-site to the client boardroom, where they professionally delivered the project status.

As a project manager for several years, I worked my way to VP. I have the perfect example of keeping calm and leveraging feminine power. One day, I arrived at a job site to be greeted by all the workers sitting on the sidewalk in front of the building. This job site was one of those where we had to use an external elevator from the ground to the floor where we were installing a trading room. They were sitting on the sidewalk instead of working inside because there was a dispute between the electrical and floor contractors about who would pick up the debris outside the equipment room. This issue occurred most days on most sites, and as the intermediary between all the trades and the client, I insisted on the clearly-delineated contract terms. On the sidewalk this day, the floor supervisor, clearly annoyed by my authority, pulled me aside and pointed to the top of the building where our external elevator stopped, indicating a skid of bricks. He said, "See that skid of bricks up there? It's got your name on it," as an all-out threat. I turned my head to the right away from him to collect myself, and I spotted a New York City street-long dumpster with my last name on it. I pointed to the dumpster and told him, "Funny, that has my name on it too." It was amazing how quickly everyone returned to work, and word spread around NYC not to mess with me.

A leader must inspire, motivate, walk the walk, and—dress the part! I typically wore statement jewelry like the beautiful necklace in this essence, hand-crafted for me by Raquel Castillo-Gamino, assembled from parts and pieces given to me by a dear friend, now departed.

The other photo is a story and a half. I always wanted a red Corvette, I mean, always. This beauty is my third Corvette. We won't talk about #2 as it was a 13-year horror, but this 2017 Sting Ray Grand Sport manual transmission with seven forward gears and five driving modes is my baby. First time in my life, I picked every element of the car's design, including the red-on-red interior, and was along for the whole manufacturing journey.

The fellowship around Corvettes started in 2000 when a co-worker fellow Vette person invited me to join the Corvette Club—talk about FUN. Road trips, car shows, obstacle course driving, and lots of camaraderie. Plus, I went to Corvette racing school in Pahrump, Nevada, where, believe it or not, I was constantly being urged to go faster. Humorously, the exact opposite of what the adorable Arizona State Trooper said when he pulled me over doing 104 mph. It was 116 degrees when he finally turned on his lights and got me to notice him behind me, so I pulled over. I'd been driving red Corvettes for almost two decades, and this was about to be my first ticket.

When the Trooper appeared at the passenger-side door, he said, "If you had kept it under 90, I could have given you just a warning."

"Had I known! It was just too tempting, though! I was looking ahead at this beautiful flat, straight road, and cars were getting out of my way and letting me fly by. So no, I didn't see you behind me for ten miles!"

"I was there!"

"Obviously! Here you are!"

Oh well, another credential to my resume. Arizona online driving school graduate. Come to find out, it's all in the computer, so you cannot dispute your speed, nor can the officer ignore it. I wondered what was taking so long, longing to get back on the road and go fast again. I still had some Arizona highway left until I reached California. The officer's dispatchers were in fits of laughter over my license plate (WIZE AZE), which prolonged the ticketing process. I asked for a humor concession, but no deal. Oh well, the experience wound up being a pleasurable and memorable moment.

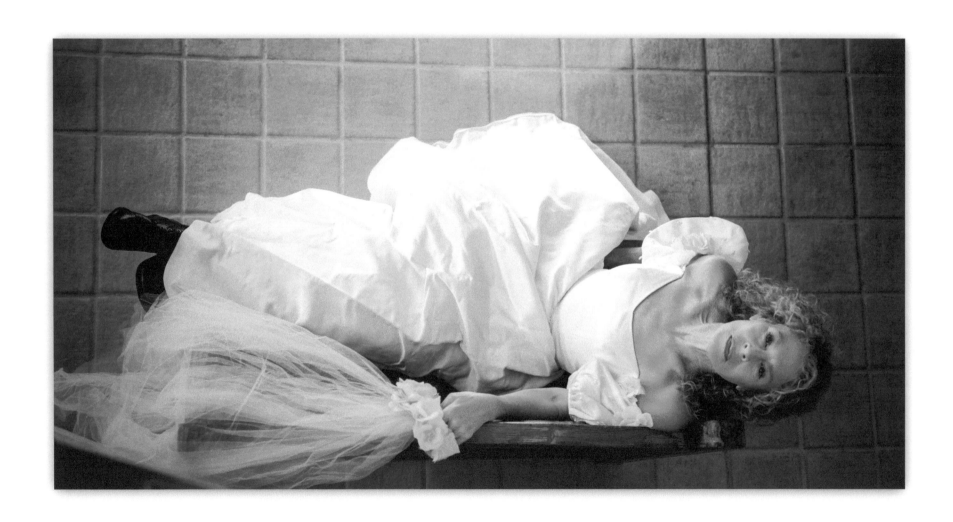

Dark Side – Constrained

Essence is Dark Side
My Version of Dark Side is Constrained

I am going to be right up front here—I DO NOT LIKE BEING TOLD WHAT TO DO—however, ask me, and I will do just about anything for you. My mother was inordinately unreasonable, and when I would question the why of her demand, the answer would invariably be, "Because I said so." Then I would go to my dark side, "constrained," overly controlled, and stuffing all the anger and frustration. I will share the serendipitous story of this dress a little later in the book. This photograph depicts my silent, constrained, determined self—over time, I have learned that going inward is fine, but stuffing anger and frustration is deadly.

I have mindset commitments that help me to get out of my Dark Side and into my Essences:

Listen more than I talk
Read more than I watch
Learn more than I teach
Laugh more than I cry
Love much more than I don't

The Trench coat and umbrella in the water symbolize how I now deal with my dark side. Instead of being constrained, I found an alternative. Now I consciously employ humor to keep the emotions out in the open to be seen and dealt with and by doing "The Right Wrong Things" to move forward creatively. It is so important to let go of the feelings that don't serve us—of course, much easier said than done. My mother's anger clung to me—yes, hers, because, as it turned out, it was never mine—for years and years until she passed on my birthday after staying alive for five days with sepsis. I experienced such liberation, releasing the pent-up childhood anger. As children, we don't know better. In truth, her dying on my birthday was a passing of the wand—I was now officially the Matriarch. That pothole-filling moment is about carefully preserving your power: it's like virginity, since you can only lose it once.

"Do the best you can until you know better. Then, when you know better, do better."
—Maya Angelou

And don't be afraid to ask for and find help; it is an act of courage, not cowardice.

Inner Child – Buoyant

Essence is Inner Child
My Version of Inner Child is Buoyant

In stark contrast with my Dark Side, my inner child has always craved Joy, that reckless abandonment you get while jumping up and down on a bed. Unfortunately, joy eluded me for the better part of my life until 2008, when my dear friend Carole Smith invited me to be on a book panel with the wonderful author and speaker Bonnie St. John with *Live Your Joy,* her first book. I clearly remember the first call as I stood at the kitchen counter while we took turns defining what joy looked like for each of us. This question silenced me—if you know me already, it was uncharacteristic for me to be without words. I had no idea, nor had I even ever thought about joy. It was a whole new concept for me. By definition, I certainly had joy in my life—my son was 15 and has always been the light of my life. But living in joy was a whole new breed of cat, and, truly, that was the first day of my ongoing quest to understand, find, and live my joy.

Up to that point, it was all about coulds, shoulds, and woulds; you know, all that stuff we are "supposed" to do. There had been, along the way, lots of therapy, counseling, group work, seminars, coaches, hypnosis, clearings, and many more attempts to get help toward clarity that I can't even recall but nothing to that point that focused on just living in and with joy.

Unfortunately, we humans don't come with an operating manual. Coming from a loveless childhood, I can remember very little, so it was the beginning of a committed full-on project to find me. More therapy until I couldn't stand to hear my story anymore. Spiritual explorations, meditation, Human Design (the game changer), IT Factor On-Camera training (another game changer), astrology, numerology, chakra clearings, akashic record reading, sound baths, and Hot Yoga (because being strong in the body enables clearer thinking). Developing a solid and committed, yep, several-times-a-week-come-hell-or-high-water yoga practice paved the way to achieving my ultimate goal of clarity and self-familiarity.

It turns out joy was there inside all the time. Spoiler alert—it is that simple, being present in the moment is true joy. Bliss is the activation of potential. Flash forward to the present, and the reason I am writing this book and telling my story is so that you and, hopefully, generations that follow can be encouraged and guided to finding IT—JOY—sooner in life than my 70 years and thereby enjoy it sooner and for many more years to follow.

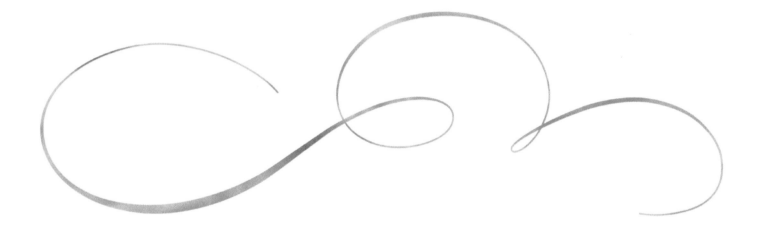

Passion – Animated

Essence is Passion
My Version of Passion is Animated

Facial expressions, hand gestures, and full-body movements are how I express my passion for everything. The act of becoming animated is a true bellwether for me. It's as if no thinking is involved like a mysterious hand takes control of all the cells in my body. I am a water baby, happiest always in and around H2O, particularly the ocean. Fountains, running water, waves, and cross-currents mesmerize me. Guessing I didn't always know that, but somehow, the universe kept putting me in the right places and with the right people with boats and beach access. Now my intention is to own some beach property so that upon exiting the front or back door, my feet find the sand with ocean water nearby. Setting clear intentions is the key to having them come to pass. That's how I intentioned myself out of the corporate world after 40 exciting years, in exactly the way and time desired. I pitied the manager who severed me; he had no idea I had scripted my entire exit. I wrote my intention on May 15th, 2011: "I will be paid to leave British Telecom within two years." May 15th, 2013, was my release date, and there was a full double rainbow to seal the deal. Talk about affirmation!

My red Corvette and our current fabulous home are what I intended precisely. For years we had considered remodeling our first home; however, to get to where we wanted to be, the only recourse was to tear it down and start over. No way. So, one day, the contractor and architect were over, and I said, "You know what, guys? We are moving." My husband included, they all snapped their heads in my direction. "Yes," I said, "We are moving, and we will stay in the neighborhood."

The contractor, a super nice human, was relieved because he knew he would never be able to give me what I was seeking. So, I began cleaning out, and every time Dale (my husband) came home, I was cleaning out another closet, drawer, or shelf. "What are you doing?" he would ask, to which I replied, "We are moving! Get your butt out in the garage and start clearing your stuff." "But we haven't found a place to move yet," he would say. "I know, but we will, so please clean the garage."

Within a few weeks—seriously, less than a month, our dream home walked into our living room. While hosting a cabi clothing party at my home, a realtor from another town showed up. Why? Because she was showing houses in our neighborhood. "For real," I said. "Where?" "One block over. Want to see the flyer?" "Yeah!!!" It was love at first sight. I copied the paper, gave it to my husband and son, watching a football game on TV, and said, "This is the house we are moving into—go take a look." That was Sunday, and on Thursday, we were in final negotiations.

P.S. Guess who was still cleaning out the garage the day we handed over the keys.

All the fruits of clear and profound intentions happily ensconced our family in this marvelous structure for the last twelve years. Dream it, and write it down—it's a powerful combination!

Dramatic – Exuberant

Essence is Dramatic
My Version of Dramatic is Exuberant

I live in a no-drama zone. I avoid drama at all costs, yet dramatic is another story entirely. Dramatic architecture, extraordinary splashes of color, sharp angles, and asymmetric cuts in clothing have always made my heart beat a little faster. Exuberant—every single word that describes or explains this word (cheerful, sparkling, animated, irrepressible, abundant, thriving, and upbeat) is who I am and aspire to be. Conversely, every word that is the opposite is who I am not and wish not to be (gloomy, meager, dour).

When I was a little girl, yikes, ten years old, I saw the 1960 movie *Pollyanna:* "A young orphan Pollyanna (Hayley Mills) believes life's most difficult problems can always be surmounted by a positive attitude and pragmatism. But when she moves in with her dour aunt (Jane Wyman), she is introduced to a range of disheartened folks who challenge her upbeat outlook. But, not to be discouraged, she sets to work spreading hope and good cheer." The scene in the movie I keep top of mind is where she puts a crystal in the window, which draws the attention of a sad old man to the brilliance of the prisms of light that spread all over the room. It GLOWED. The older gentleman lit up, and so did she.

My core value is GLOW, and my sole purpose is to help people find creative ways to express their inner GLOW, so they can stand in their power as I do in mine! That is the way I live my life; GLOW allows me to be, think, learn, dress, and explore with a Dramatic flair and Exuberant energy.

Understanding what makes you tick is paramount to living your essence.

Humor – Mischief

Essence is Humor
My Version of Humor is Mischief

Humor and Mischief are like peanut butter and jelly—they naturally go together. Throw in an ounce or two of cleverness, and it can be pretty entertaining. I have way too many stories to back up this theory. Here are a few of my favorites.

We all remember times when we couldn't help entertaining ourselves, possibly at the chagrin of our target. My first year at Kent State University, where I transferred after my freshman year at Quinnipiac College (now University) in 1970; yes, during the KSU events, four dead in Ohio—I was there. Yet from August to May 2nd, my dorm mates and I cut up BIG time.

From the moment we met, my best girlfriend was Joanie Soeder, a gal from Chester, Ohio, my dormmate in the room across the hall. Joanie would take me home for long weekends, and I even got to spend a Thanksgiving with her and her family as my home was an eight-and-a-half-hour drive away in New Jersey. Joanie and I would hit the refrigerator as soon as we walked in the door to lay out the table with rye bread, liverwurst, Limburger cheese, and spicy mustard. Oh, and sliced raw onions. Joanie's mom would come home from work, yelling from the driveway that she could smell us.

After the first school semester, Joanie's two roommates left school, leaving her with a triple. The ever-resourceful Joanie disassembled the single bed and loaded it under the bunk bed lower tier, and took up residence on the top bunk leaving lots of enviable floor space.

Hmmm, what to do with all that space? Stuff it! KSU was a big weekend commuter school, so I requested everyone in the hall to return each weekend with the Sunday newspapers claiming I had a project that required massive amounts of newspaper. For several weeks the piles grew. Oh, by the way, Joanie was so kind as to let us store the stacks in her room, you know, the room with all the new-found space—until, that is, one evening when she was out on a date. I marshaled all the willing co-conspirators to help me ball up these massive amounts of newspaper and toss them back into her room. Yep, we stuffed the room—floor to ceiling, wall to wall, front to back until you could barely open the door a few inches. Then we silently waited in my room until she came home, and we heard her shriek, "BOOM BOOM"—my Ohio nickname (more on that in a bit). We popped into the hall, and all fell on the floor hysterically laughing, including Joanie. The next day, Joanie and I unstuffed the room and put all that paper down the incinerator chute—yep, three-foot flames were coming back up and out of the chute door on the third floor, and the lobby of Olson Hall filled with smoke. Our house mother, Mrs. Eschler, a lovely aging gracefully gal, was starting to sense we were going to be a handful, oh, and we did not disappoint.

Joanie's revenge was several nights later when I came back into my room, the one across the hall, and so as not to disturb my two roommates, did not put on any lights. I quietly got undressed and was about to fall into bed when I realized there was no bed!! My bed had been dissembled and reassembled in the shared bathroom down the hall. Apparently, in addition to the same co-conspirators involved in the newspaper caper, the RA (Resident Advisor) was in on it too, all thinking that giving me a dose of my own Mischief with a sign on my bed in the bathroom, "Spring had Sprung" would curtail my antics—nope.

We had tall, like up to mid-chest height built-in drawer units in the dorm rooms—recessed in the wall, two sets of five drawers each, made of heavy, sturdy blond wood.

The gals next door would return every Sunday night with loads of food and put the food on the top of their drawer unit, which backed up to ours. So naturally, we had to welcome them back, and the drawer slam races would commence. We called them "sh#t" slam races because that was what we yelled when the race began. You cannot imagine the cacophony we were able to create lying on the floor on our backs, feet braced on the slightly open drawers, and racing to close them. We expanded this concept dorm wide and had every door on all three floors open only to be "sh#t-slammed" in perfect sequence, one door and floor at a time. The resonance snaked through the dorm and out into the quad because one go was never enough—we did the sequence bottom to top and top to bottom three times. Mrs. Eschler was undoubtedly getting a major headache; may she rest in peace.

One last dorm story. The sisterhood of the traveling tassel. Where we came up with stuff is still a mystery. Sunday was usually the day we were bored, and being in Ohio, it was probably cold and wet—I came to know there were two seasons, Winter and August, so we entertained ourselves.

For some reason, this particular Sunday, we glanced through the Sunday paper and saw a full page of ads for stripper clubs. Joanie, Darla, and I thought it would be great fun to adopt stripper names and have them be our incognitos. I was Boom Boom Boomski and hence shortened to Boom Boom, which still serves me today when playing on social media with my Millennial friends. Boom Boom and Mil Mil, cute, right?

Then came the tassel, from where or how is still unknown, 50 years later. That tassel wound up in suitcases, greeting cards, small packages, cars, and pants pockets. The fun part was targeting one of the three of us and having it show up when least expected, making it incumbent upon the recipient to pass it on stealthily to one of the others—not sure who was the last holder of the tassel. Still, it served our friendships well and with honor.

Romantic – Glamorous

Essence is Romantic
My Version of Romantic is Glamorous

When most think of something or someone being romantic, it typically has at least one of the following components: candles, soft music, words of love, and adoration. Hmmm—not for me. The element of surprise is my idea of romance because it has confidence all over it. Trusting yourself enables Glamorous, which is being and feeling attractive or appealing in an exotic or exciting way. When someone profoundly knows themselves, they need little or no propping up from others because they have done the work to align with their purpose, so they have a strong sense of self and willingness to be themselves. I find romance in that aura. It seems to me that being romantic is an inside job because if you don't love yourself, it isn't possible to be romantic with or love another.

I am Glamourous by nature; I didn't know that for a long time—in fact, for decades—but I sure do now. When you recognize what energy and situations you are most natural in, you have discovered your Essence, making life so much easier. Flowing, Glowing, Romantic, and Glamorous—living your best life on your terms, "Hot cha cha"—that's the Golden ticket (as in Brendon Burchard's book *Life's Golden Ticket: A Story about Second Chances).*

I have read, listened to, attended, and experienced many guides on this journey to self-awareness, from Abraham Hicks to Amy Cuddy, from Rick Levine, astrologer, to Keri Murphy, on-camera message expert, to Baeth Davis, Human Design master, and Simon Sinek's TED Talks, from woo woo to science with inspirational voices in between, have all influenced me.

Sensual – Coquette

Essence is Sensual
My Version of Sensual is Coquette

Not going to lie; I have had a lot of conflict with being sensual because, like most, I always associated sensuality with sexuality. However, while their definitions are a hair's breadth of difference, they are separate yet equal.

Sensual is an adjective relating to or involving gratification of the senses and physical, especially sexual, pleasure. Sexual is also an adjective, in this case, pertaining to the instincts, physiological processes, and activities connected with physical attraction or intimate physical contact between individuals.

In other words, you can have one without the other.

I promised you the story of the wedding dress in the Dark Side Essence. It all began when I saw Goldie Hawn star in the movie *Private Benjamin.* As the story opens, she is a run-away bride and had on the most fabulous Anna and the King of Siam dress. I rewatched the movie credits more times than I can count and could not find any mention of the dress! Undeterred, I kept hunting. I was in an excellent place because I was in New York City. And yet, I still came up empty-handed until one day, I saw a side panel in *The Wall Street Journal* with an advertisement for gowns by designer Ada Athanassiou. Never being shy about something I wanted, I called her immediately, told her the story, and guess what. It was her dress! It turns out that when they wardrobed the movie, they bought it off the rack at Bergdorf Goodman's, so no credit was given.

Yes, she had the dress design, it was still current, but she couldn't sell one to me because she only sold wholesale, and I was retail. Finally, after several rounds of questions, it became apparent that my girlfriend, Angela Oliveri, who was in the garment industry, could make the purchase. So, we went arm-in-arm to Ada's studio, and she custom-made my dress for me. That was in 1981, and I am thrilled beyond all measure that it still fits. This dress is testimony to two of my pet phrases when making purchases: first, you have to love it—not like it, love it, and that way, you always will. The second is to buy good, get good. I don't care if you're shopping in a thrift store or a high-end boutique. You need to know what good is because quality counts.

I find being a Coquette, a woman who flirts, is sensual. Why? Because it feels good and ties back to romantic and glamorous because being a coquette requires wit and confidence. I charm the little children I teach how to swim. Making other humans feel good about themselves is a large part of my purpose because it is a win-win. My dear friend Harvey Jaffe always said, "Love is the only thing that the more you give, the more you get."

Harvey also said, "If the Rock hits the pitcher or the pitcher hits the rock, it will still be bad for the Pitcher." Pretty sure he was referring to a glass pitcher, but the baseball metaphor works too.

Harvey and I were friends from the time we were two years old. I'm not sure why I chose this page as the right place to insert those Harvey-isms, but it felt good.

Braced – Spontaneous

Essence is Braced
My Version of Braced is Spontaneous

Braced is preparing oneself for something difficult or unpleasant. When I began exploring the Braced essence, I had no idea what that meant. Since we rarely use the word outside architecture and engineering, you may also wonder about its meaning in the essence context. So, the definition of Braced I initially pursued is an action, a verb to make (a structure) firmer with wood, iron, or other forms of support.

The personal essence resonated for me in the synonyms: support, shore up, prop up, hold up, buttress, carry, bear, underpin, strengthen, reinforce, and fortify. What props me up, reinforces, and strengthens me is being Spontaneous—in other words, shooting from the hip and having the confidence to honor my instincts in the moment. It can be in action or words, and the latter either gets me into trouble or can be pretty funny. For example, my late first father-in-law, Charlie Casalino, took delight in calling me his outlaw daughter (versus in-law) and couldn't quite figure out why my Italian cooking and entertaining skills were above par. He would always ask, "Where in Italy are you from?" to which I would always reply, "Northern," until one day he asked me, "How far North?" being of Northern Italian descent himself. My response was, "Russia," and we laughed till we cried. Although that story is decades old, it still cracks me up.

My husband, Dale Lewis, always says, "If you want to be a better skier, ski with a better skier," which means to me, "Upping my ante is my key to growth and how I remain Braced."

Spiritual – Simple

Essence is Spiritual
My Version of Spiritual is Simple

Where to begin on this Essence of being Spiritual? It is, at the same time, fixed and dynamic. I believe Spirit and Spiritual are part of our physical incarnation, as I subscribe to the principles of Human Design wherein, we obtain our star seed or design 88 days before we are born and then, upon the moment of birth, our personality. One is the physical DNA, and the other is spirit; we are a complete package, as within, so without, as above, so below. Astrology, Human Design, Numerology, I Ching, and all of the ancient concepts based on the universe are ours from the get-go. Yet, some of us wind up chasing what feels right according to our perspective based on the environment of our upbringing and community.

I have become a spiritual creature by getting to the basics—truth, kindness, understanding—live and let live. However, I am not always able to maintain these Simple principles. At different junctures, my perspectives have changed, influenced by people, current events, and my surroundings. As one of my early mentors, Vince Corica, shared, Miles' Law states, "What you see depends on where you sit." For example, a CEO and a mailroom clerk in the same company typically have very different perspectives. However, it gets Simple when FEAR (false evidence appearing real) is removed from the equation. Except in the case of red flags, those warning lights that go off when something or someone doesn't feel quite right. The only word of caution I'd like to share is that a red flag will always be a red flag, so please don't ignore it.

This book comes from my insatiable desire to remove FEAR and instill Trust in as many lives as possible in this lifetime. Especially for those younger than me, whether by a few weeks or many decades, so they can live life freely and with joy as if they had the accumulated wisdom of my now many years.

Achieving a unique style is a journey. A journey filled with compare and contrast, before and after, bold and shy, confident and maybe not so confident, do I or don't I, what was I thinking and I totally nailed it moments.

All because of what we decided or had decided for us to drape our bodies, hair, and face with, all in an effort to be ourselves. If only we came with an operating manual. Indeed, we do come with an operating manual. We were born at a unique moment in time, in a specific place, with the stars and planets in precise degrees of placement in the astrology of that very moment. It was and will forever be our very own. Even twins are unique as they have moments of separation, distinguishing them from each other.

Getting dressed has evolved parallel to my understanding of who I am as a unique, sovereign, autonomous being and letting go of what people say.

The journey to "unique" is not for the faint of heart. It requires gladiator fortitude. I think of one of my swim students, a beautiful young creature who is the middle child bracketed by an older and younger brother. She always wore one favorite bathing suit, although it was stretched out and too small, and she had many alternatives at home. That bathing suit was her battle gear, as were several dry land outfits. You can imagine this would cause a certain amount of strife before any activity that required her donning clothing to participate in, especially for her dear mother, who would repeatedly suggest new options, plead, and finally acquiesce to her daughter's favorites.

It became crystal clear that this little lady knew her unique style. Her tenacity carried over into her determination to swim when she said, "I'm going to do it," she did it. And when someone else gave her a little challenge, she would watch them and then go right in the water and do what they did, often better.

This swimmer's example illustrates how we are who we are from the inside out. Everything is possible given the opportunity to develop that self-knowing, which her mother was so brilliant at allowing and encouraging.

We live in times that make it easier to be cookie-cutter copies of one another than to pursue and express our uniqueness. I have been a crusader for individuality, which brought me to study Human Design. Life gets much simpler when you understand the blueprint and actual weave of your fabric. It's like getting the keys to a treasure chest or secret closet where the holiday gifts are hidden. Once you discover your uniqueness, it makes it easy to wrap the package—you—with the colors, textures, designs, angles, volume, and sleekness that complements and enables your uniqueness in your outer expression.

Most summers, I teach young children how to swim, which is one of my most gratifying endeavors because it is an exercise in trust. Their parents trust me with their children, and I teach the children to trust themselves by curing them of their fear of being dropped in water too deep for them to stand in. It is a miraculous transfer of trust enabled by a few words whispered in their ear: "I will never drop you or let you go unless you tell me to." And then I deliver on that promise.

That memorable little swimmer, wearing her magical bathing suit, the one she chose and felt confident in, went from the shallow water to the deep with trust and ability. Guess what. Once she started swimming in the deep end, she began wearing some of the other bathing suits in her drawer and changed up her other outfit options outside the pool. It was noticeable as she transformed into her uniqueness like a butterfly evolving from the pupa of the caterpillar.

May you find that uniqueness in yourself and highlight it with an accessory, a specific color, shape, or design—a trademark. Identify your special "bathing suit" and use it as your touchstone to achieve all the uniqueness you were born for—Spiritual, plain and Simple.

As mentioned in the Inner Child Essence, when I was on the book panel for author Bonnie St. John with her book *Live Your Joy,* the outset of the discussions, I knew I was going for a deep dive. I couldn't answer the first simple question on the panel: "What is joy for you?" Bonnie suggested I think about how I felt about Beau. When I told her how I felt, I lit up and spoke of him with pride in every way—a feeling of great pleasure and happiness. Bonnie helped me identify my feelings as joy. It soon became evident that this initial step began a lifelong journey to find out more about what joy means to me. Twenty years later, so many pieces make more sense, knowing that joy is Spiritual. It is trusting myself with myself and participating in life with reckless, fear-less abandoned dreaming—now taking action is Simple.

Inner Male – Gladiator

Essence is Inner Male
My Version of Inner Male is Gladiator

Still Untamed after all these years when it comes to what I am passionate about—fairness and injustice. "Gladiator" originates from the late Middle English word in Latin, gladius, "sword." It could be my Holocaust DNA lineage as I have been very clear about what is worth fighting for, just like a man in ancient and modern times who trains to fight with weapons against other men or wild animals in an arena.

I am a Gladiator for my only child Beau Saul-James Lewis, underdogs, people with disabilities, and Ignorant Injustice. Growing up in the 1950s and 1960s was foundational as a time of tremendous awakening, specifically around women's rights and racial equality.

My childhood home was anything but nurturing, yet my father was a renaissance man in many ways and had the honest-to-God League of Nations in his circle of friends. We called every one of them Aunt or Uncle. As the eldest of four children with many expectations and responsibilities placed upon me, I often rebelled; however, the perspective afforded me was limitless. As such, I had no filters regarding the inequality of human value. Everyone was important in their own right, and if they couldn't defend themselves, I stood up against their aggressor. Most of the time, the aggressor was my mother—a pretty unhappy woman with a penchant for interrogation and corporal punishment. After she would make fun of me when I suggested she speak to my siblings first, I always got between her and them, even while she was swinging the belt.

Another instance was in sixth grade with a classmate's older sister who had polio. One day, in the schoolyard, when a bully was making fun of her, the hair went up on the back of my neck, and nothing could stop me from interceding. I knocked him to the ground even though he was bigger than me. The funny thing is, I never got in trouble with my teachers, Miss Barbarisi or Mr. Richmond, or even the school principal, Mr. Lyons—all pretty gladiatoresque names, don't you think?

Another time more recently, my Gladiator came out, this time for Beau who was spending an inordinate amount of time with math in his first year of college. From the time he was an infant, he was fascinated with airplanes, and it was one of his very first spoken words, "Airplane." We spent weekends at Santa Monica Airport watching planes take off and land. There was never a question about what he wanted to be when he grew up—Pilot. After watching him pour over his math homework until the wee hours one too many nights, I asked if I could talk with him about it. I said, "Do you have to take all this math to be a pilot?" He responded, "No, it's for mechanical engineering." I said, "Then why?" He replied, "Because if I don't make it as a pilot, engineering will be my fallback." "Oh, for goodness' sake, do you want to build or fly the planes?" He went to class the next day and dropped the math because I was a Gladiator for his dream of being a pilot.

Fast forward eleven years later, and guess who is now a USAF c130 Hercules pilot? Yep. Being a Gladiator means flying without a safety net, going for it, whatever IT is, which doesn't require battle. I can accomplish anything I want by standing for what I believe in with my Gladiator's shield (grace) and armor (elegance). In my case, it is high fashion and style in words and appearance.

So that's what 70 looks like, which can be at any age. By embracing an understanding of who you are and what you are here to do and living it is ageless and the real deal—the Essence of Aging Gracefully.

Grace – Comfort

Essence is Grace
My Version of Grace is Comfort

You can always squeeze in another pair of shoes. Shoes have forever been my go-to when I needed a wardrobe pick-me-up. Since they are not dependent on your body size, a new pair of shoes is an easy way to satisfy that yen for something new to wear. I also feel that way about lipstick, particularly shades of red to match my Vette. So, head-to-toe quick fixes. I joked during the shutdown of 2020 that earrings were the new shoes because of all the zoom calls and the focus on waist-up visuals. Finding comfort in your skin, environment, and all those moments where you show up is so much easier with grace.

We just completed editing the Essences and this quote showed up in my email. Go figure.

Your life is your story. Write well. Edit often.
—Lisa Nichols, Author, Motivational Speaker

Postscript

Several significant epiphanies have crystalized since I began writing this book in 2020. First, I established my triangle, the most structurally sound shape for my values of living. Kindness, bravery, and integrity are the three points of the triangle.

With these three values in place, I can easily say yes or no to people, places, and expenditures. In the old days of punch cards for computers, there were always some cards we called discard-eligible, meaning they weren't necessary to the overall outcome of the data run. Likewise, my values make situations and choices very easy because the discard-eligible ones don't fit inside my triangle. So, I'm out if there isn't bravery, integrity, kindness, or any combination of the three.

Throughout the last many years, I felt like I was wandering in the dark, looking for my community, those folks with whom I could grow, serve, and bond. I am creating my own family. While the members don't necessarily know each other, I hold each in a special space as they do for me. Thankfully my chosen family is growing and thriving.

I knew I was home the first time I walked into Keri Murphy's Inspired Living Brilliant Event six years ago. I breathed in the energy in the room like the scent of freshly baked chocolate chip cookies. Our chance meeting has grown into a respectful partnership just like the childhood I didn't have.

Soon after I met Keri, I met Baeth Davis, who is a force of nature. She challenged, provoked, and encouraged me in personal growth I had no idea was possible. If I had any delusions of sugar-coating my life, she blew them out of the water early on. A true mentor in every sense of the word, Baeth is my natural choice to write the foreword for my book, and I'm honored that she accepted.

My Rotary community has allowed me to be part of a club of service-oriented generous folks who accomplish amazing feats of tear-filled joyful giving. I am grateful for the persistence of Gwen Vuchsas in getting me to join The Rotary. Throughout grade school, no one ever invited me to be part of a sorority, clique, cool kid parties, or gang of friends. Therefore, this gathering of my chosen family is a new and exciting chapter of my life in the community. So much so that I am hoping to be appointed Honorary Mayor in the coming years.

Another discovery was my One Word core value from Rich Keller, who I initially met through Keri Murphy. I aligned his visual appearance with his 2023 TEDx Talk theme and he rocked it. Then, he guided me to my One Word core value in his SCORE program. After reading my SCORE workbook, he said, "Your One Word jumped off the page—it's GLOW. Even my wife saw it."

Immediately I rebranded using my One Word and now approach situations, people, and life with GLOW at my core. GLOW fits inside my triangle beautifully. Can you see it shimmering in the middle of kindness, bravery, and integrity? I sure can, and I see it all the time. I share it a lot when someone invites me to, and I'm very generous with it because, according to Harvey Jaffe, and as we know, love, as well as glow (isn't glow just a form of love?), the more we share, the more we get.

May this book be well read, broadly shared, and the principles embraced. The journey to self is an adventure; the longer you live, the more experiences you have to compare and contrast, and the more beautiful your life can be.

I hope I have given you plenty to think about and take action on because you are in control of yourself, so take the reins of your life. Please, think for yourself, dress for yourself, and take care of yourself, and your life will be vibrant and fulfilling. My mission is to help you feel great about yourself…after all, to GLOW—not a lofty goal because living well is our God-given right. However, as in my early experience, if you don't have the right mentor or one close at hand, you will always have me just a book's reach away.

Happily-ever-after is a work in progress, and now you have a partner.

About The Author

Hand Me Downs to High Fashion, Wall Street to LA

Bobbie Casalino-Lewis: The Expression Expert grew up in the New York metropolitan area during an era of significant change, shaping her view of the world and embedding a clear understanding of the importance of how one visually presents themselves. "Fashion is what you wear. Style is how you wear it." That mantra was the backbone of her notable success in all the high-level corporate leadership roles she held. Now she employs those same experiences, talents, and perspectives in reworking lives by re-tooling wardrobes. She is all about identifying and revealing her client's confidence, presence, and positivity. Bobbie's mission is to encourage, embolden, and enable others to have "Wordless Introductions" that speak loudly and proudly of who they are, what they stand for, and where they will make an impact. A Spiritual Intuitive Expression Expert and Motivator, Bobbie is hired by confident leaders who must show up powerfully in the world. She's transformed Thought Leader Baeth Davis and is the "Go-to Expressionist" for Keri Murphy's IT Factor On-Camera training. Her work has helped clients renew relationships, gain confidence and become client magnets. In addition to individual clients, she aligns speakers' expressions with their TEDx Talk themes. Wrapping people in their message is her specialty.

Bobbie is passionate about bringing out everyone's inner Glow so they stand in their true essence. Whether appearing on stage in front of hundreds or interacting in day-to-day activities, it is abundantly clear that our outer self-expression must align with our authentic essence. Bobbie is a role model and expression expert for good reason: she walks her talk. Her clientele includes executives seeking to have more impact in the boardroom, professionals who want to improve their connection with clients, athletes who want to up their game, Domestic Engineers who want to be role models for their children, and workplace recruitments who wish to make a confident impression to insure their first season of success. She specializes in dressing you for the day you envision in alignment with your message and purpose. Her services extend from intuitive personal style assessments to motivational speaking and full-service VIP makeovers. Bobbie's clients concur that how they show up in the world dramatically changes after she works her magic and brings out their inner Glow.

In Memoriam

Harvey Jaffe

Before we close, let me tell you a little bit about my friend Harvey. Aside from being across-the-street neighbors from when we were two years old until we both went off to college, we were best friends. We would have battles about who was on which side of the center line of the street we lived on when we had one of our spats. They could have been about any number of things, but most assuredly, benign. Harvey was a grade behind me, and yet he incorporated himself into my grade. So, my friends were his friends, and his friends were my friends to this day. He did not have an easy time growing up. He was the youngest of three boys and had an extremely abusive father and an overwhelmingly loving mother. Harvey's favorite meal was roast duck, which my mother would prepare for him every so often to his delight. He was the fifth child in our home. He and my father were great friends, and neither let an opportunity to bust me slip by. However, they both stood by me through thick and thin. Harvey was my supervisor when I tried to iron the curl out of my hair and used Uncurl to accomplish the same.

As years progressed and our lives unfolded, the synchronicities between Harvey and me were never-ending. His wedding, without any former knowledge, turned out to be the day after mine, his firstborn was on my first wedding anniversary, and we eventually lived in adjacent towns in New Jersey. In addition, I am the godmother to his three children from birth, Matt, Kari, and Marissa.

There are way too many stories over the sixty-plus years of our friendship to even begin to recount. However, Harvey being a master storyteller, I can assure you the retelling would take almost as long to tell as it was to live. He was always my rock and loved calling me Sheba.

During the last thirty years of our friendship, we settled on opposite coasts and kept in touch. I would frequently visit friends on the east coast, and spending time together was always on the agenda.

November 8th, 2017, was one of those days. I flew into Newark Airport ahead of schedule, picked up a vehicle, and met him at his apartment. He had been out all day, dealing with his progressed health issues, being driven around by his new and best friend, Malik. Harvey and I visited for a bit and then set off in my rental van to do a couple of errands before heading to dinner. Of course, we had a tug-of-war over where to eat, one of many comedies we perpetuated over the years. He suggested a corner restaurant not far from our final errand, to which I said, "Absolutely, no." Then we set out to retrace some of the drives we had done in high school in search of a mutually-agreeable location, laughing and remembering our youthful antics until I saw a restaurant named "Chakra" and said, "Let's go there." He said, "No, it's too expensive." I said, "I'm buying!" And he persisted on the too-expensive part. Finally, I said, "Okay, we'll settle this. Call them and see if they serve roast duck." Guess where we ate that night. However, the evening turned out to be much more eventful than I could have ever imagined.

The ambiance was that of the Arabian Nights. We sat in a giant U-shaped booth with sheer draping in the four corners. The restaurant wasn't very busy as it was a weeknight. Harvey loved his Caesar Salad with lots of dressing. He always ordered what he called a "wet" salad. This waiter got it right. No small feat when addressing Harvey's palette. Next came The Duck, a ritual of savoring every bite.

We were having our normal Harvey-Bobbie conversation, which was him telling me what to do and my pondering his words of wisdom until his voice shifted tones, and he said several things that he'd never said before. They were all intensely meaningful, and I'm glad I was paying attention because, after the last bit of advice, he turned his face back to his food and said, "I don't feel very good." His shoulders butter-flied, his chin dropped to his chest, and he was gone.

It is still very clear what happened afterward. In the next booth, there turned out to be eight critical-care nurses who pulled him from the booth after I punched his shoulder and shook him, telling him to stop fooling around. They began CPR. I ran to the front of the restaurant and had them call 911. But I knew he was gone. And so, he was.

People materialized from the bar and other tables, and I was grateful they surrounded me. It was all very surreal, as you can imagine. But in that moment of shock and awe, somehow, I knew this was his choice. Think about it: He was having his favorite meal with his favorite friend, doing his favorite thing, which was telling me what to do. To this day, when someone says, "Oh my God, that must have been so devastating," I reply, "It was, but still quite magical because I know he chose me, and he chose his time."

In speaking with Malik the next day, he told me about how Harvey had rushed him around all day so as not to be late for me. Now we knew why. So, Harvey and my dad are having a pretty fun time out there in the universe, and they often visit me to let me know that they are still here for me. Losing Harvey was a double-edged sword. He was my memory bank and remembered things I either blocked or chose to forget. He took my history with him. I had always depended on him to tell me when, who, or what about stories and incidences from my life. In retrospect, the good, bad, and ugly information, in the wrong hands, could very well come back to bite me. So now my secrets are safe, Harvey's at peace, and life very much goes on.

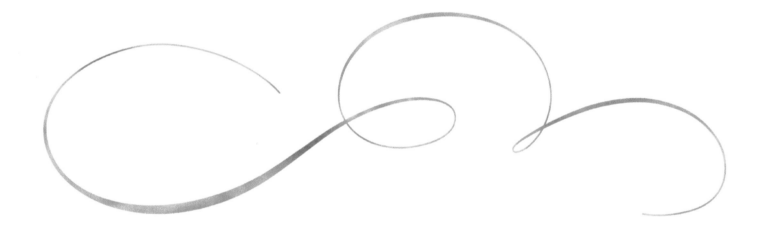

Printed in the USA
CPSIA information can be obtained
at www.ICGtesting.com
LVHW061549240124

769531LV00022B/92